The praying mantis is an amazing insect. You can find it in most places around the world, except where it is very, very cold. Why is it called a praying mantis? Because when it hunts, it folds its front legs under its head. It looks as if it's praying.

Just a little closer.

Praying mantises didn't always live in the United States. P. Mantis, the praying mantis that lived in the author's yard in Connecticut and inspired this book, was related to mantises that came from China to Pennsylvania more than a hundred years ago.

Adult praying mantises eat just about anything they can catch. That means that live insects like flies, moths, crickets, mosquitos, grasshoppers, spiders and other mantises had better watch out! Even small animals such as frogs, mice and birds can become a meal for a mantis.

How do praying mantises catch their prey? They use their lightning-fast front legs, called raptorial legs. These legs have rows of sharp spines that hold prey tightly.

Yum!

Praying mantises use camouflage to hide from predators. Color is one type of camouflage. Praying mantises are usually brown or green, but they can also be white, pink or yellow. They also sway or rock to look like a leaf or a stick blowing in the wind.

Can you see me?

My Awesome Summer
by P. Mantis

PAUL MEISEL

Holiday House / New York

For Peter, Alex, and Andrew

The publisher would like to thank Louis N. Sorkin, B.C.E.,
American Museum of Natural History,
for his expert review of this book.

Copyright © 2017 by Paul Meisel   All Rights Reserved
HOLIDAY HOUSE is registered in the U.S. Patent and Trademark Office.
Printed and Bound in September 2018 at Toppan Leefung, DongGuan City, China.
The artwork was created with acrylic ink on Strathmore paper, digitally enhanced.
www.holidayhouse.com   7 9 10 8 6
Library of Congress Cataloging-in-Publication Data

Names: Meisel, Paul.
Title: My awesome summer, by P. Mantis / Paul Meisel.
Description: New York : Holiday House, [2017] | Audience: Age 4-8. |Audience: K to grade 3.
Identifiers: LCCN 2016027035 | ISBN 9780823436712 (hardcover)
Subjects: LCSH: Praying mantis—Juvenile literature.   Classification: LCC QL505.9.M35 M45 2017 |
DDC 595.7/27—dc23   LC record available at https://lccn.loc.gov/2016027035
ISBN 978-0-8234-4006-1 (paperback)

MAY 17

I was born today! It's a beautiful, sunny spring day!

MAY 18

It was so crowded in the egg case. Really, really crowded—
me and around 150 praying mantis brothers and sisters.

Here I am.

I don't have any wings yet so I can't fly.

MAY 19

It's okay that I can't fly.
The bush I was born on has
aphids all over it. Yum!
Soft and delicious!

I'm down here.

MAY 24

Some big birds landed near me. I did my cool trick, pretending to be a stick blowing in the wind.

They flew away.

Uh—oh!

JUNE 2

All the aphids are gone. I'm hungry.
Growing so fast!

I ate one of my brothers.
Okay, maybe two.

JUNE 4

I ate another brother.

And one of my sisters too.
I grew again. I shed my skin.

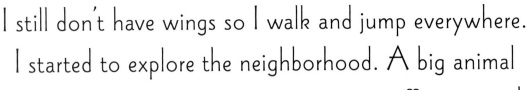

JUNE 27

I still don't have wings so I walk and jump everywhere.
I started to explore the neighborhood. A big animal
came sniffing around.

I did my cool trick again.
You can't see me. I'm a stick.

For a pipsqueak I've
got some sharp teeth.
My razor arms
are superfast too!

A grasshopper hopped
next to me. I grabbed
him before he could
say Jiminy Cricket.

JULY 17

I grew some more. Shed my skin again.
Still can't fly, so more walking,
jumping, exploring.

Sorry, brother.

JULY 19

Ran into one of my brothers.

He tried to eat me.

So I ate him.

JULY 27

Sometimes I like to hang out upside down. Mostly when I
shed my skin, but other times for fun. I'm getting pretty big now.
Unlike other insects, I can turn my head to see what's behind me.
Hello!

JULY 29

Praying?
Yeah, I'm praying.
Praying something tasty comes
along that thinks I'm a stick.

AUGUST 2

I grew again. Shed my skin again.

I hung upside down
to get my old skin off.
I felt a little naked until
my new skin hardened.

AUGUST 9

Ahhh. I love the summer!

Long hot days. Cool nights. I like to hide in the shade and eat bugs near the flowers. I chewed the head off a bee. Not my favorite.

AUGUST 15

Finally! I can fly! Almost got eaten by a bat.
Landed on a branch and made like
a stick until it flew away.

AUGUST 25

I nearly walked into a spider's web. Spiders
scare me. This one wanted to eat me.
I jumped away as fast as I could.

Grew again. I shed my skin too.
Last one for the summer.
I forget. I think it's 8 or 9 times.

SEPTEMBER 25

Fall is here. There's a chill in the air.
I'm looking for the perfect branch.
Not very hungry.
Moving slowly now.

OCTOBER 14
I found it! The bush where
I was born. I laid eggs. Put foam
around them.

It hardened and made an egg case.
Hundreds of praying mantises
will be born in the spring.

OCTOBER 17

I'm going to lie down now and take a long nap.
Good-bye!

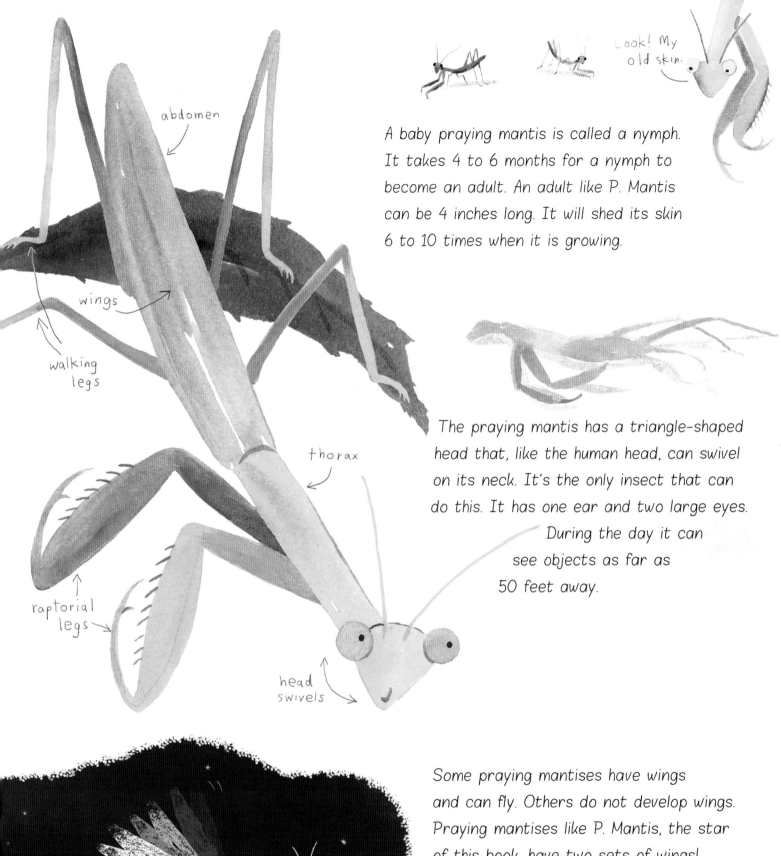

Look! My old skin.

A baby praying mantis is called a nymph. It takes 4 to 6 months for a nymph to become an adult. An adult like P. Mantis can be 4 inches long. It will shed its skin 6 to 10 times when it is growing.

abdomen

wings

walking legs

thorax

raptorial legs

head swivels

The praying mantis has a triangle-shaped head that, like the human head, can swivel on its neck. It's the only insect that can do this. It has one ear and two large eyes. During the day it can see objects as far as 50 feet away.

Some praying mantises have wings and can fly. Others do not develop wings. Praying mantises like P. Mantis, the star of this book, have two sets of wings! Males are lighter than females and can fly longer distances.

P. Mantis would not have been able to defend herself very well from a bat, spider, bird, frog, or lizard that might have wanted to eat her. Praying mantises try to defend themselves with their sharp forearms, or they stand up tall and spread their arms to look bigger. They even make a hissing sound. But against larger, stronger predators, they are pretty defenseless.

In colder climates like the one where P. Mantis lives, females lay up to 300 eggs. They cover the eggs with foam that becomes a hard, protective egg case, called an ootheca. Adult praying mantises don't survive the winter. But their babies hatch in the spring. Then the cycle begins all over again.

WEBSITES:

http://aggie-horticulture.tamu.edu/galveston/beneficials/beneficial-20_mantid_praying_mantis.htm

https://extension.umd.edu/hgic/insects/predators-praying-mantid-mantis

https://www.stlzoo.org/animals/abouttheanimals/invertebrates/insects/grasshopperskatydidscricke/prayingmantis/

GLOSSARY

aphid: a small bug

egg case or ootheca: a case that holds eggs